Working with Big Data and Machine Learning
Part - I

SRINIVAS V V

ISBN-10: 1973894912
ISBN-13: 978-1973894919

DEDICATION

This book is dedicated to my parents, for their kindness and passion, and for their endless support; their selflessness will always be remembered.

CONTENTS

ACKNOWLEDGMENTS

I would like to express my happiness and gratitude to everyone who saw me through this book; to all those who provided support, talked things over, read, wrote, offered comments, allowed me to quote their remarks and assisted in the editing, proofreading and design.

1 BIG DATA

Has your organization taken full advantage of the new data landscape? Are you keeping pace with the rapid growth of new data sources available to you? Our world is increasingly driven by data. The amount of data grows exponentially with years.

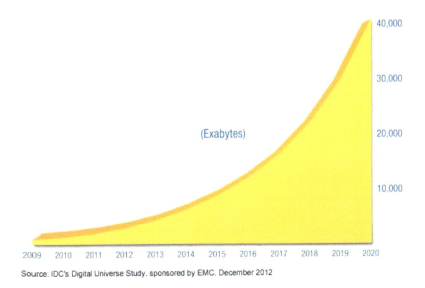

Source: IDC's Digital Universe Study, sponsored by EMC. December 2012

So what data are we talking about? What data grows exponentially? Here data refers to social data concerned with peoples likes, dislikes, preferences; scientific data which refers to medical information, climatic data, demographic data etc.; banking and e-commerce data related to financial information, consumer purchase.

E-Commerce Data

Banking

Social Media

Medical & Scientific data

The data mentioned is of little use if it is not converted into useful information. This has led to the growth of a new field of study called Big Data or Data Analytics. Big Data is not just data, but processing of large volume of data and converting the data into some useful information.

Now that we know what is big data, the next thing is how to get big data? There are many ways of getting data, one of the most common methods is traffic to a particular site. Blogs and sites created now a days comes with user login which happens mostly using third party authentication such as Facebook, google, twitter, live id authentication or using custom authentication. When such authentication is provided using OAuth authentication, it is easy to obtain users consent to obtain information on users likes, preferences. Similarly analytics sites such as google analytics and Bing analytics provide insights into which region users tend to visit the site, what is the duration of users visit on a particular page, what are the preferences of the user. Similarly medical data is obtained on sites that provide medical information such as disease, causes and symptoms and prevention. Financial data such as market trends and analytics can be obtained by collecting market data over a period of time; and Scientific data can be collected the specific fields. The overall idea is data is collected over a period of time.

So we have setup ready to collect data, but how useful is this data collected? Not very useful. And how big is the data? During initial setup of the application, the data remains small, but as we collect more and more information the data grows. It grows in size from KB, MB, GB, TB.

kilobyte	KB	10^3
megabyte	MB	10^6
gigabyte	GB	10^9
terabyte	TB	10^{12}
petabyte	PB	10^{15}
exabyte	EB	10^{18}
zettabyte	ZB	10^{21}
yottabyte	YB	10^{24}

| Kilobyte (KB) | Megabyte (MB) | Gigabyte (GB) | Terabyte (TB) |
| 1KB = 1024 B | 1MB = 1024 KB | 1GB = 1024 MB | 1TB = 1024 GB |

The chart shows the various sizes of data

As the size of data grows, it has led to the advancement of hardware. The picture above shows floppy disks which were few KBs replaced by CDs of few MBs replaced by DVDs and USB sticks of few GBs followed by hard disks of TB to PB capacity. Here we see that data grows exponentially, whereas the hardware growth is becoming more linear. In order to overcome this limitation, we come up with networked or clustered machines, each machine containing petabytes of storage to cope up with storage and computation of big data. Now we have the technology to store large volume of data, do we have the compute power to process such large volume of data into useful information? The answer to the question is yes.

Earlier the processing of large volume of data was done by increasing the clock frequency of a processor. The next stage was to increase the number of cores within the processors. Next was to increase the number of processors. Now that we have reached a limit on the processing power of single machine, we have moved to processing on multiple machines.

This chapter will not discuss in detail the evolution of processor technology, but will discuss the different techniques used in processing big data. Now we know the different systems and architectures that were used for processing data, we will be discussing on how the processing of data was done.

The data obtained from front end and middle tire systems are classified into structured data and unstructured data. Structured data is again classified into relational structured, tabular structured data.

Relational structured data are those stored in databases. The data in relational databases have primary and foreign key relationships and are mostly processed using a data warehouse. An example for relational structured database would be SQL Server Management studio, Oracle SQL developer, where the data is stored in tables with primary and foreign key relationships. The key disadvantage of using relational data is the amount of data the database engine can process. Relational database makes use of clustered and non -clustered index for faster accessing of data. A clustered index is one in which the index directly points to the data, whereas a non-clustered index is one in which the index points to the address where the data is stored.

SQL Server Management Studio

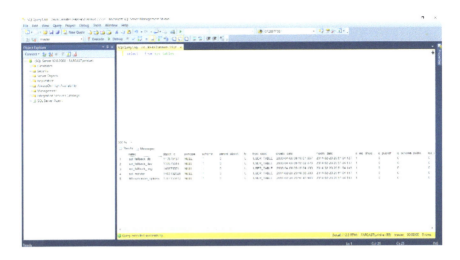

Oracle SQL Developer

Recent trends show many variations of relational structured data, wherein data is directly stored in json format in Mongo DB, neo4j stores data in the form of graph.

```
switched to db test
> create collection("mycol")
2016-03-21T10:39:38.864+0000 E QUERY    SyntaxError: Unexpected identifier
> test.createCollection("mycol")
2016-03-21T10:40:05.433+0000 E QUERY    ReferenceError: test is not defined
    at (shell):1:1
> db.createCollection("mycol")
{ "ok" : 1 }
> db.mycol.insert({name:'SRI', age:25})
WriteResult({ "nInserted" : 1 })
> db.mycol.find().pretty()
{ "_id" : ObjectId("56efcfb55626495358f95c8d"), "name" : "SRI", "age" : 25 }
>
```

Tabular structured data is a form of table storage which does not contain any relationships. Tabular form of storing can be faster for processing large volumes of information in comparison to relational database. The key point to note is that the information stored should not contain any relationships and should be flat in structure. The tabular storage contains row and partition keys for faster access to the indexed data. An example for tabular storage is azure table storage which can be accessed from storage explorer.

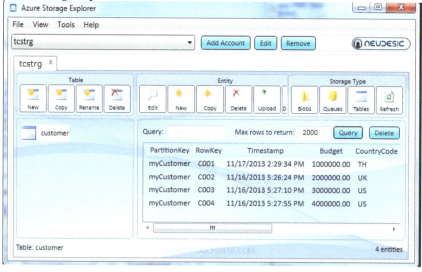

Unstructured data is generally data stored in flat file storage. The data that is stored in unstructured data does not contain any relation, does not contain any index. The data stored is totally raw data.

Now that we have discussed the different types of data that is available, how do we manage when data grows huge? If the data is stored in relational or tabular storage, the process of increasing the size of the database or the tabular storage to accommodate the incoming data is called scaling. In case of relational database there are different types of scaling namely: Scalable

Shared Database, Peer to Peer replication, Linked servers and distributed queries, Data dependent routing.

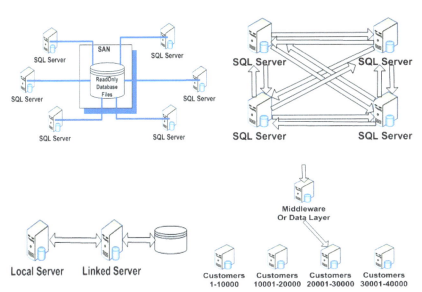

Here the first image shows Scalable Shared Database, which can be used only in case of data warehousing. Peer to peer replication can be used only in case of low update operations. The two most common methods of scale out are linked servers which are also known as functional area wise partitioning wherein the tables are placed on different servers based on the functional area and accessed using linked queries. And in case of Data dependent routing, data is divided into either vertical partition or horizontal partition and queries are routed to the appropriate server based on the incoming query. All the methods discussed are kind of complex and requires more time to scale out.

In case of tabular storage the scale out process is either horizontal partitioning or vertical partitioning. The easiest of scale out is for unstructured data. It only involves increasing the storage size. In our case adding one more server to the cluster refers to scale out.

We have finally understood the different types of data and how to store data as it grows into huge volumes. The next important thing is to convert this data into useful information. Some of the common applications of data processed are trend analytics, understanding people sentiments, generating reports, machine learning and data modeling, predictive and preventive diagnostics, market analysis etc.

Till now we have been discussing about data that is transactional in nature. Before the data is converted into useful information and displayed into report, some transformation needs to be performed. This transformation is performed at a data warehouse level. Here data warehouse can be any one of the storage types such as relational database or a tabular storage or a processed file. The process of loading data from a transactional database [OLTP – Online Transactional Processing System] to a data warehouse [OLAP – Online Analytical Processing System] is called as ETL [Extract Transform and Load].

Some popular tools that perform ETL transformation are Microsoft Business Intelligence Studio, IBM Info Sphere, Informatica, Oracle Data Integrator.

Once the process of ETL is complete Machine Learning or OLAP can be run on top of the data warehouse to get useful insights into the data. Some of the existing OLAP tools available in market are Microsoft Cubes, Oracle OLAP.

2 HADOOP

What is Hadoop? It is a name given to a set of libraries, that together form a framework allowing processing of huge data across multiple computers. Some of the key providers of this framework are Amazon Web Services, Microsoft HD Insight, Cloudera, Dell, EMC^2, Hortonworks, IBM, Apache.

Now we saw what is Hadoop and the key providers of Hadoop. So what it is made of? Hadoop consists of a distributed file system [HDFS]. This distributed file can run on a single machine or can span across a large cluster. It is a highly scalable, high throughput distributed file system that forms the heart of Hadoop. A resource manager called as YARN that takes care of resource cluster resource management and job scheduling across clusters and a MapReduce framework for processing of data across clusters in parallel.

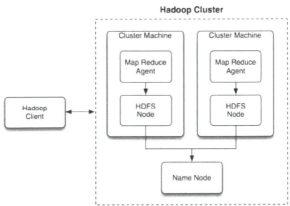

The figure above displays a simple hadoop cluster, consisting of the HDFS, a single Name Node, Secondary Name Node and Data nodes [Cluster

Machines]. The figure given below shows that after setingup HADOOP, the command start-dfs.sh is for starting the HDFS and the command jps displays all the processids of Name Node and DataNode.

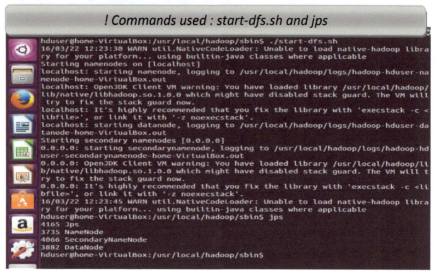

! Commands used : start-dfs.sh and jps

Now that we know the block diagram of HDFS, we need to understand in detail the architecture. The HDFS makes use of master slave configuration. The Name Node acts as master managing the file system and access to file system by clients. The Data Nodes are connected to the local storage of each machine and handle the read and write requests to the local storage.

The image shows the command used in accessing a simple Hadoop file system. Most of the commands used by Hadoop are simple bash commands e.g. ls (directory listing), cat (to read contents of a file), mkdir (creating a directory), rm (to remove a directory).

! Commands used : hadoop fs -ls /folder

The list shows commands used when accessing hdfs file system. appendToFile, cat, chgrp, chmod, chown, copyFromLocal, copyToLocal, count, cp, du, dus, expunge, get, getfacl, getmerge, ls, lsr, mkdir, moveFromLocal, moveToLocal, mv, put, rm, rmr, setfacl, setrep, stat, tail, test, text, touchz.

Till now we have been looking at the key component of HADOOP, which is the DFS. The next and the most important component in HADOOP is the resource manager. HADOOP makes use of YARN resource manager. YARN resource manager has a central Resource Manager and multiple Node Managers. The image given below displays Node and Resource Manager.

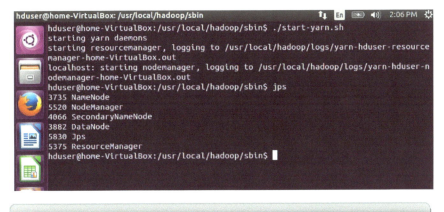

! Commands used : start-yarn.sh and jps

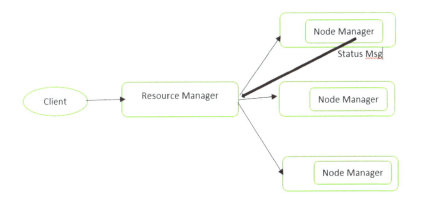

YARN makes use of a capacity scheduler, which consists of a set of queues and set of resources. Each queue is associated with a set of resources so that there is a control over the resources available.

We will be discussing MapReduce framework and how to implement MapReduce and its application in other chapter. Till now we have discussed the architecture for Hadoop components. Now we need to know how to setup Hadoop. In this chapter we will be discussing the setup with respect to Ubuntu (Linux). The setup can consist of a two configurations, namely Sandbox configuration wherein the entire name node, data node, and resource managers are configured on a single machine. The second approach consists of multiple machines and setting up in a cluster environment.

We will first discuss the setup for single node cluster or a Sandbox configuration. Use the following commands to perform a single cluster configuration or sandbox configuration.

1. Setup java

```
sudo apt-get install default-jdk
```

2. Creating a dedicated user hduser for ssh into localhost

```
sudo addgroup hadoop
sudo adduser –ingroup hadoop hduser
Set the password to: hduser
sudo adduser hduser sudo
```

3. Setup ssh and sshd (ssh-daemon) to access localhost

```
sudo apt-get install ssh
su hduser
ssh-keygen -t rsa -P ""
cat $HOME/.ssh/id_rsa.pub >> $HOME/.ssh/authorized_keys
ssh localhost
```

4. Download hadoop and extract hadoop using tar command. Copy the extracted hadoop folder to /usr/local/hadoop. If the folder does not exist create one.
5. Add the following environment variables to bashrc

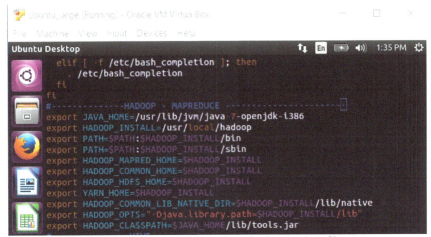

6. Execute the following command after closing bashrc file.

source ~/.bahsrc

7. Add the following JAVA_HOME code to hadoop_env.sh

8. Add the following lines of code to core-site.xml

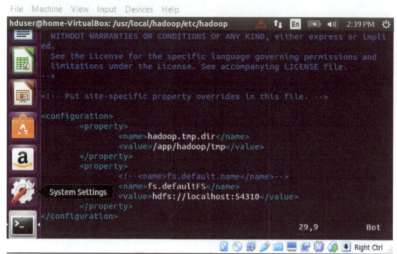

9. Copy /usr/local/hadoop/etc/hadoop/mapered-site.xml.template to /usr/local/hadoop/etc/hadoop/mapered-site.xml

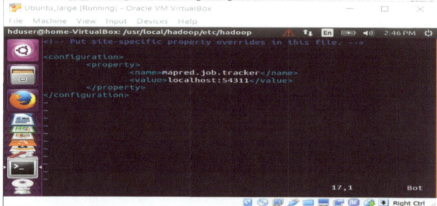

10. Create two folders namely using the following commands
    sudo mkdir -p /usr/local/hadoop_store/hdfs/namenode
    sudo mkdir -p /usr/local/hadoop_store/hdfs/datanode
    sudo chown -R hduser:hadoop /usr/local/hadoop_store
11. Configure hdfs-site.xml

```
hduser@home-VirtualBox: /usr/local/hadoop/etc/hadoop        ↑↓  En      ◀))  2:52 PM
<!-- Put site-specific property overrides in this file. -->

<configuration>
        <property>
                <name>dfs.replication</name>
                <value>1</value>
        </property>
        <property>
                <name>dfs.namenode.name.dir</name>
                <value>file:/usr/local/hadoop_store/hdfs/namenode</valu
e>
        </property>
        <property>
                <name>dfs.datanode.data.dir</name>
                <value>file:/usr/local/hadoop_store/hdfs/datanode</valu
        VBOXADDITIONS_5.0.14_105127
        </property>
</configuration>

                                                        17,1            Bot
```

12. Format the hadoop file system

> *hadoop namenode -format*

Now that the setup is complete, we can start using hadoop using the commands given in figure 2.2. Till now we have discussed the single standalone cluster setup. The setup is mostly used in case of development purpose, and hence known as sandbox environment. In case we need a proper multi-cluster setup, then we need to follow the instructions given below.

Create two virtual machines which can communicate with each other, with the single cluster or sandbox setup, as shown above. Once the setup is done, setup the slave nodes ip address on the master machine. In the figure given below the left side shows the master machine with ip 192.168.56.103 and slave machine with ip address 192.168.56.104.

On the master machine in /usr/local/hadoop/etc/hadoop/slaves file enter the master machines ip address and the list of all the slave machines ip address as shown in the figure.

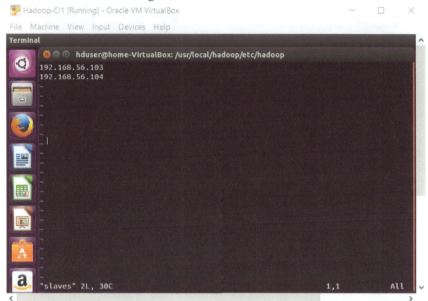

Modify the core-site.xml. Here replace hdfs://localhost:54310 with the ip address of the master machine.

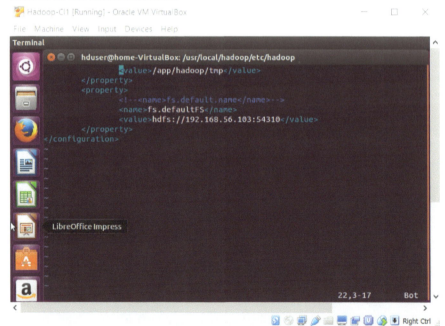

Similarly replace localhost with the master machines ip address in mapered-site.xml and dfs replication to 2. In case master machines IP address is not mentioned in multi node cluster environment, an error will be displayed while accessing the file system using "hadoop fs -put" command.

Format the name node using the following command.

> hadoop namenode -format

Now on starting dfs and yarn, the namenode and resource manager starts on the master system and the datanode and node manager starts on the slave.

Note: If the setup is copied using vhd and if there are exceptions related to datanode such as "there are 0 data nodes running", try deleting the data folder present in /app/hadoop/tmp folder and recreate the folder using the following command

```
sudo rm -r /app/hadoop/tmp
mkdir /app/hadoop/tmp
chown 750 hduser /app/hadoop/tmp
```

Similarly clear the datanode folder present inside hadoop_store folder using the following commands mentioned.

```
rm -r /usr/local/hadoop_store/hdfs/datanode
mkdir -p /usr/local/hadoop_store/hdfs/datanode
```

Now format the namenode using the command mentioned in the previous page and start the namenode, datanode, yarn job and task trackers.

Following are some of the popular DFS commands that can be used using Hadoop:

```
                    !Commands
hadoop fs -ls /
hadoop fs -mkdir /folder
hadoop fs -put sourcefile /folder
hadoop fs -get source /folder
hadoop fs -cp /folder1 /folder2
hadoop fs -rmr -skipTrash /folder - recursive deletion
hadoop fs -cat /folder/file | less [q to exit from less]
```

The commands mentioned above are the same as linux shell commands. For accessing the DFS from datanode use the following command:

```
hadoop fs -ls hdfs://<<master>>:54310/<<folders>>
```

3 MAP REDUCE

Map Reduce is a program containing two functions namely, mapper and reducer. Map Reduce helps in processing large amount of data across multiple machines. So, why do we need such a program? The answer to this question is when the data becomes too large to process, processing on a single machine or node becomes time consuming.

Now that we have mentioned, the time taken to process on a single machine becomes time consuming and we need to make use of multiple machines to process the data. The immediate thing that comes to mind is why Map Reduce and what are the other methods to process data faster. There are programming languages such as MPI (Message Passing Interface), CUDA parallel programming and computing which does computing across multiple machines; MapReduce is one such technique for parallel processing.

The main difference between MPI and MapReduce is that MPI is mainly for faster computation and can be used for synchronous and asynchronous result processing, the key disadvantage being data movement across nodes and data in memory processing. Map Reduce is slower compared to MPI but the key advantage is scalability of data nodes, and data localization and data movement between memory and disk. It depends primarily on application to application whether to use MapReduce or any other parallel technique. This book covers MapReduce in the upcoming sections.

Map Reduce always works in <key, value> pairs. In order to understand the working of MapReduce let us consider a simple example of Word Count program as shown. The wordcount program consists of three methods namely a main method, a TokenizerMapper method, IntSumReducer method.

```
public class WordCount {
  public static class TokenizerMapper extends Mapper<Object, Text, Text, IntWritable>
    private final static IntWritable one = new IntWritable(1);
    private Text word = new Text();
    public void map(Object key, Text value, Context context
                    ) throws IOException, InterruptedException {
      StringTokenizer itr = new StringTokenizer(value.toString());
      while (itr.hasMoreTokens()) {
        word.set(itr.nextToken());
        context.write(word, one);
      }
    }
  }

  public static class IntSumReducer
      extends Reducer<Text,IntWritable,Text,IntWritable> {
    private IntWritable result = new IntWritable();
    public void reduce(Text key, Iterable<IntWritable> values, Context context
                    ) throws IOException, InterruptedException {
      int sum = 0;
      for (IntWritable val : values) {
        sum += val.get();
      }
      result.set(sum);
      context.write(key, result);
    }
  }

  public static void main(String[] args) throws Exception {
    Configuration conf = new Configuration();
    Job job = Job.getInstance(conf, "word count");
    job.setJarByClass(WordCount.class);
    job.setMapperClass(TokenizerMapper.class);
    job.setCombinerClass(IntSumReducer.class);
    job.setReducerClass(IntSumReducer.class);
    job.setOutputKeyClass(Text.class);
    job.setOutputValueClass(IntWritable.class);
    FileInputFormat.addInputPath(job, new Path(args[0]));
    FileOutputFormat.setOutputPath(job, new Path(args[1]));
    System.exit(job.waitForCompletion(true) ? 0 : 1);
  }
}
-- INSERT --                                                          25,4
```

The WordCount program shown above.

3 MACHINE LEARNING

Machine Learning refers to identifying a model and predicting the solution for a given problem statement. There are number of machine learning libraries and programming tools available in the market. In this Chapter we will look at what is machine learning, some of the different types of algorithms and how to use machine learning using R, Apache Mahout and Azure Machine learning techniques, SPARK MLib, Python Machine Learning library.

The machine learning library that can be used with Hadoop are Spark MLib and Apache Mahout. These are highly scalable machine learning libraries that makes use of machine learning algorithms.

Machine learning is classified into 3 major types of algorithms namely, Supervised learning, Unsupervised learning and Reinforcement learning.

Supervised Learning

In supervised learning, there is a training process. The training is done on test data, and based on the training, a model is generated. Using the model generated, the test data is evaluated for desired output. Most of the prediction algorithms make use of supervised learning wherein, based on the past data, the future is predicted. The supervised learning is further classified as Classification algorithms and Regression algorithms. A Classification Algorithm as the name suggests, helps the given input to be classified as option A, option B or option C. Classification Algorithms deal with groups or binary values. Whereas a Regression Algorithm deals with real values like money, quantity etc.

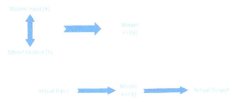

Unsupervised Learning

In the case of unsupervised learning, there is no model data. Based on the incoming inputs, the model needs to be derived. Unsupervised learning is mainly used in case of large data sets. Unsupervised learning is classified into Clustering and Association algorithms. Clustering algorithm as the name implies, grouping of incoming data into sets. Association algorithms are similar to clustering, the key idea being associate a particular input a specific rule.

Reinforcement learning, takes input, creates a model, generates the output. The output is taken along with the input for modifying the function, to get better accuracy on the output. The complexity of these algorithms are higher than normal algorithms.

So now that we have seen there are so many algorithms available, there are certain questions that needs to be answered. Do we really need Machine Learning for our application?, how to arrive at which Algorithm to use?, how to use the algorithm using a particular programming language?

Machine Learning is needed mostly to predict the future based on past inputs or present inputs or both, some of the examples are:

(a) Unmaned cars, that take the input parameters from the road (such as near by vehicles, obstacles) using sensors (IoT), pass them to a learning algorithm in order to apply breazks or stear left or right.

(b) Tsunami warning and prediction systems, that take in recent changes in geology based on sensors (IoT) and send data to learning algorithms to provide warnings.

(c) Trend analysis, based on past data predict future trends (eg. Stock market, Property market, Education analysis Pass percent every year, Health care – probability of person becoming diabetic based on past records, Sales or product for future based on current trend, Sentiment analysis on a particular area etc…).

Based on the examples stated above, Machine Learning algorithms start with sample data and build on top of it, to improve itself, to predict accurately. So the Machine learning algorithm which is a black box takes in set of inputs (few independent inputs and few dependent inputs – e.g. In property market, Year and Locality are independent variable, price of flat in the area is dependent variable) and produces probability as output. So the first question, does our application require machine learning?, the answer to the question is, most normal, simple applications don't, but if it is a revenue generating or critical application then having machine learning implemented on top of the application gives an edge over the competitors.

The next important question to address is, there are lots of Machine Learning algorithms out there, which one to use? The best answer to this is, if it is enterprise application and you have the data in large volumes, then based on the sample data, a data scientist can predict the accurate model/algorithm to use. But if you are interested in knowing which algorithm to use, most of the applications fall under one of the category.

(a) Data that can be classified into two sides of a function. E.g. Linear regression, nonlinear regression. Here the input parameters to the system are mostly, a single independent parameter and set of dependent parameters and the output is a probability. The threshold is the line shown below and the coordinates fall on either side of the threshold.

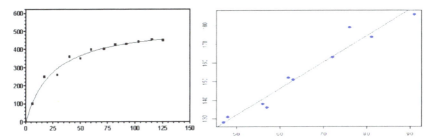

(b) In case there are more than two sides as described above, they are classified under clustering or grouping or association algorithms. The example shown below shows grouping of similar items.

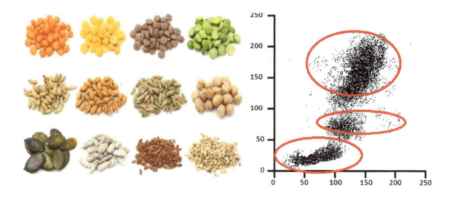

(c) The other commonly used algorithm is, the decision tree based algorithms. The output depends on the present state of the machine and the current input. An example would be unmanned car, where the present state is running straight and no obstacles, and the input to it is an obstacle in center as a result the decision would be to apply break; in case the obstacle is towards left then the decision would be to move right, and if the obstacle is in right then the decision would be to move left.

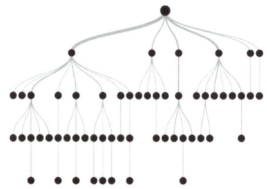

The next step shows the list of Algorithms available. Most of the Classification algorithms mentioned are also capable of regression. If you are not able to classify the algorithm into one of the categories shown above it is better to try the algorithm on the problem and find the accuracy of the algorithm. Below is a R language example where we use linear regression and random Forest for the same problem statement and find the accuracy for each of the algorithms.

In the table below we list all the algorithms available in Machine Learning.

Algorithm Class	Algorithm Name
Classification	Logistic Regression
	Native Bayes
Regression	Linear Regression
	Survival Regression
Decision Tree based algorithms	Random Forest Algorithm

Azure Machine Learning Algorithms

Now that we have looked at the what is machine learning, classification of machine learning algorithms and the different types of machine learning algorithms, the next thing that we will look at is different programming languages and how to use machine learning using the programming languages.

Machine Learning Workflow

A Workflow is key to machine learning. The workflow consists of the following steps namely:

1. Get the data
2. Ask the right questions and come up with the problem statement
3. Prepare the data [Data cleanup]
4. Select the Algorithm
5. Train the model
6. Test the model
7. Get the result

If the obtained result is not effective, then add more data or change the algorithm to obtain better results.

Machine learning using R

In order to understand machine learning using R language, we should know certain basics of R language. Download R from cran or use RStudio for development purpose.

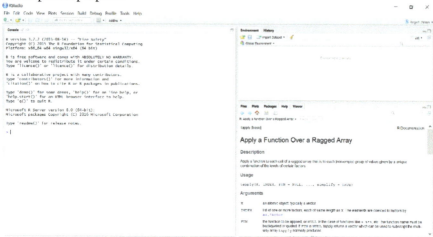

Use the Machine Learning WorkFlow to correlate the steps given below with the workflow. The first step is to find out the right question and what is the end goal that we are trying to achieve.

The problem statement given below and the solution are taken from Pluralsight. The link for the same is provided. https://app.pluralsight.com/library/courses/r-understanding-machine-learning/table-of-contents.

Here the problem statement is to find out all the flights that are getting delayed with an accuracy of >=70%. Delay here refers to arrival delay where flights taking more than 15 mins of time than the expected time.

The table consists of the following columns DAY_OF_MONTH, DAY_OF_WEEK, UNIQUE_CAREER, AIRLINE_ID_CAREER, TAIL_NUM, FL_NUM, ORIGIN_AIRPORT_ID, ORIGIN_AIRPORT, ORIGIN, DEST_AIRPORT_ID, DEST_AIRPORT, DEST, DEP_DEL15, DEP_TIME_BLK, ARR_TIME, ARR_DEL15, CANCELLED, DIVERTED, DISTANCE

	DAY_OF_MONTH	DAY_OF_WEEK	UNIQUE_CARRIER	AIRLINE_ID	CARRIER	TAIL_NUM	FL_NUM	ORIGIN_AIRPORT_ID	ORIGIN_AIRPORT	ORIGIN	DEST_AIRPORT_ID	DEST_AIRPORT	DEST	DEP_DEL15	DEP_TIME_BLK	ARR_TIME	ARR_DEL15	CANCELLED	DIVERTED	DISTANCE
2	1	7	AA	19805	AA	N3CGAA	307	11292	1129202	DEN	14107	1410702	PHX	0	1100 1159	1328	0	0	0	602
3	1	7	AA	19805	AA	N3CGAA	307	14107	1410702	PHX	14057	1405702	PDX	0	1500 1559	1653	0	0	0	1009
4	1	7	AA	19805	AA	N3EVAA	309	11278	1127803	DCA	13303	1330303	MIA	0	0600 0659	930	0	0	0	919
5	1	7	AA	19805	AA	N3MAAA	310	13303	1330303	MIA	12953	1295302	LGA	0	1400 1459	1646	0	0	0	1096
6	1	7	AA	19805	AA	N3FCAA	311	14107	1410702	PHX	11292	1129202	DEN	1	2200 2259	107	1	0	0	602
7	1	7	AA	19805	AA	N3LMAA	311	14747	1474703	SEA	14107	1410702	PHX	0	1700 1759	2141	0	0	0	1107
8	1	7	AA	19805	AA	N3DVAA	312	13930	1393004	ORD	13487	1348702	MSP	1	1300 1359	1523	1	0	0	334
9	1	7	AA	19805	AA	N3KCAA	313	13303	1330303	MIA	10821	1082104	BWI	0	2000 2059	2253	0	0	0	946
10	1	7	AA	19805	AA	N3DHAA	314	13303	1330303	MIA	13930	1393004	ORD	0	2100 2159	2343	0	0	0	1197
11	1	7	AA	19805	AA	N4XKAA	315	11298	1129804	DFW	14683	1468303	SAT	1	1200 1259	1423	1	0	0	247
12	1	7	AA	19805	AA	N4XKAA	315	14683	1468303	SAT	11298	1129804	DFW	1	1400 1459	1553	0	0	0	247
13	1	7	AA	19805	AA	N3CNAA	316	13303	1330303	MIA	14843	1484304	SJU	0	2100 2159	124	0	0	0	1045
14	1	7	AA	19805	AA	N3DTAA	319	14107	1410702	PHX	14057	1405702	PDX	1	1100 1159	1317	1	0	0	1009
15	1	7	AA	19805	AA	N3DTAA	319	14908	1490803	SNA	14107	1410702	PHX	0	0700 0759	1027	0	0	0	338
16	1	7	AA	19805	AA	N4YCAA	320	11298	1129804	DFW	14683	1468303	SAT	0	1000 1059	1137	0	0	0	247
17	1	7	AA	19805	AA	N4YCAA	320	14683	1468303	SAT	11298	1129804	DFW	0	1200 1259	1322	0	0	0	247
18	1	7	AA	19805	AA	N3ECAA	321	11057	1105703	CLT	11618	1161802	EWR	0	1300 1359	1509	0	0	0	529

The steps given below are generic and will be applicable for most programming languages.

Data Loading

The first step to start machine learning is to get the huge data and load csv data into a variable or table or a defined structure to operate on.

```
origData <- read.csv2('C:\users\srinive\Desktop\FlightData.csv', sep=","
header=TRUE, stringsAsFactors=FALSE)
```

After loading data check if the data got loaded into the variable. The nrow function gives the count of number of rows that got loaded into the variable.

```
nrow(origData) (or) head(origData1, 2) (or) tail(origData1, 2)
```

Data Minimization and Cleanup and Data Type Change

The other way of loading data manually is to use vectors as shown below to load smaller set of data. The following way of storing data can be used for filtering data from larger set of data.

```
airports <- c('ATL', 'LAX', 'ORD', 'DFW', 'JFK', 'SFO', 'CLT', 'LAS', 'PHX')
```

A single vector value can be obtained directly using index as shown

```
airports[1]
```

Once the entire data is loaded, smaller set of data can be extracted into variable using the operation shown below. This method helps in reducing the number of records and helps in working with major dataset and remove minor set of data or unwanted data. Select a subset of records

```
origData1 <- subset(origData, DEST %in% airports & ORIGIN %in% airports)
```

Now that a subset of data is extracted, remove all unwanted columns

```
origData1$Column <- null
```

If two or more columns contain correlated value and we do not require one of the column find the correlated columns and remove the column that you believe is not required.

```
cor(origData1[c("DEST_AIRPORT_ID","DEST_AIRPORT_SEQ_ID")])
```

Cleanup the data by removing unwanted characters such as NA, "", empty strings from rows

```
onTimeData <- origData1[!is.na(origData1$ARR_DEL15) &
origData1$ARR_DEL15!="" & !is.na(origData1$DEP_DEL15) &
origData1$DEP_DEL15!="",]
```

Convert data type as required for example char to integer if required. This will help greatly while doing computations.

```
onTimeData$DISTANCE <- as.integer(onTimeData$DISTANCE)
```

Using Machine Learning Algorithm

Once the data is loaded and cleaned we are ready for supervised learning. The algorithms are readily available and based on the outcome we identify the algorithm that is required; ref table given above. The following are the steps used in supervised learning.

1. Identify the algorithm
2. Load the library required for the algorithm
3. Divide the data into training data and test data
   [Note: Training data is used for creating the model and test data is to check the accuracy of the algorithm].
4. Call the Machine Learning Algorithms method with the required arguments on the Training Data
5. Call the predict method with the model and the test data as arguments.
6. Check the accuracy of the model using the confusion matrix
7. Represent it in graph.

The steps for performing Machine Learning are show below.

In the following scenario we can make use of Native Bayes or Logistic Regression algorithm. For better accuracy we make use of Logistic Regression algorithm.

The next step is to load the library as shown and set a random seed.

```
library(caret)
set.seed(122515) [This method is used for generating random number].
```

The third step is to create a partition of the data that we have. Here p=0.70 says that 70% of the data will be used as training data and remaining 30% will be used as test data.

```
inTrainRows <- createDataPartition(onTimeDataFiltered$ARR_DEL15, p=0.70,
list=FALSE)
trainDataFiltered <- onTimeDataFiltered[inTrainRows,]
testDataFiltered <- onTimeDataFiltered[-inTrainRows,]
```

The fourth step is to call the logistic regression method. The method can be obtained from the documentation of R programming.

```
logisticRegressionModel  <-  train(ARR_DEL15  ~  .,  data=trainDataFiltered,
method="glm", family="binomial")
```

The fifth step is to make use of the model obtained in the previous step and see the correctness with the test data that we have. This is to ensure that our model works as expected.

```
logRegPrediction <- predict(logisticRegressionModel, testDataFiltered)
```

The data obtained in logRegPrediction is not in a readable format, hence that needs to be put inside the confusion Matrix and can be analysed for correctness and false positiveness and negativeness.

```
logRegConfMat <- confusionMatrix(logRegPrediction,
testDataFiltered[,"ARR_DEL15"])
logRegConfMat
```

The screenshot of the output obtained as a result of the execution is shown below. The confusion matrix shows the Reference value with the Prediction value. Here 0 refers to the flight arrived on time and 1 refers to the flight arrived late.

```
> logRegConfMat
Confusion Matrix and Statistics

          Reference
Prediction    0    1
         0 6673 2294
         1  167  226

               Accuracy : 0.7371
                 95% CI : (0.728, 0.746)
    No Information Rate : 0.7308
    P-Value [Acc > NIR] : 0.08616

                  Kappa : 0.089
 Mcnemar's Test P-Value : < 2e-16

            Sensitivity : 0.97558
            Specificity : 0.08968
         Pos Pred Value : 0.74417
         Neg Pred Value : 0.57506
             Prevalence : 0.73077
         Detection Rate : 0.71293
   Detection Prevalence : 0.95801
      Balanced Accuracy : 0.53263

       'Positive' Class : 0
```

a. Here reference of 0 and Prediction of 0 shows 6673 which means that 6673 flights got predicted correctly as on time.

b. Reference 1 and Prediction 0 there are 2294 records which mean that 2294 flights got delayed which were predicted wrongly as on time.

c. Reference 0 Prediction1 there are 167 records which mean that 167 flights were actually not delayed but were actually predicted as delayed.

d. Reference 1 Prediction1 there are 226 records which mean that 226 flights were actually delayed and were predicted correctly as delayed.

Similarly we can change the algorithm and make use of some other algorithm and check the accuracy.

Here we make use of random Forest algorithm where we first load the library
library(randomForest)

After loading the library we make use of the method for random forest and send the data to create a model
ftModel <- randomForest(trainDataFiltered[-1], trainDataFiltered$ARR_DEL15, proximity = TRUE, importance = TRUE)
Using the model we make use of the predict function and use the test data to check the correctness of the model
rfValidation <- predict(ftModel, testDataFiltered)
rfConfMat <- confusionMatrix(rfValidation, testDataFiltered[, "ARR_DEL15"])
rfConfMat

Note here that the confusion matrix at the bottom displays the Reference which is the actual value against the predicted value. If we do a compare with the previous Confusion Matrix with the current confusion matrix, it shows that accuracy of prediction of delayed flights has improved, but on the other hand the accuracy of the prediction of non delayed flights has improved only to a small extent.

```
Confusion Matrix and Statistics

          Reference
Prediction    0    1
         0 6047 1971
         1  793  549

               Accuracy : 0.7047
                 95% CI : (0.6953, 0.7139)
    No Information Rate : 0.7308
    P-Value [Acc > NIR] : 1

                  Kappa : 0.1196
 Mcnemar's Test P-Value : <2e-16

            Sensitivity : 0.8841
            Specificity : 0.2179
         Pos Pred Value : 0.7542
         Neg Pred Value : 0.4091
             Prevalence : 0.7308
         Detection Rate : 0.6460
   Detection Prevalence : 0.8566
      Balanced Accuracy : 0.5510

       'Positive' Class : 0
```

Machine Learning using Azure ML

In order to use Azure ML go to the Azure portal, search for Add new MachineLearningWorkspace

After creating the Machine Learning Workspace, load the data required for machine learning. Here we will use the same example mentioned above for R programming language and demostrate with Azure ML.

Creating an experiment

Experiment is the workspace where the machine learning activities will take place. Click on Add new Experiment and select the blank experiment.

Loading the data

After creating the Azure ML workspace, click on the Add new button and Click on the DataSet csv file used for flight delay.

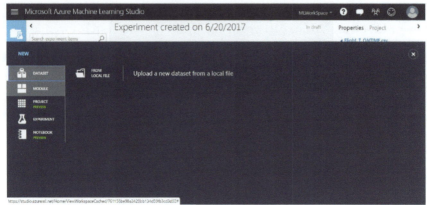

Now inside the experiment, select the Saved Datasets and Click on My DataSets and select the file that got uploaded.

From the dataset create an R script to remove end point ORIGIN and DEST airports. Have only 'ATL', 'LAX', 'ORD', 'DFW', 'JFK', 'SFO', 'CLT', 'LAS', 'PHX' the following values.

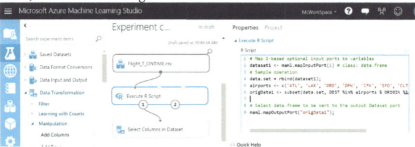

R Code

```
# Map 1-based optional input ports to variables
dataset1 <- maml.mapInputPort(1) # class: data.frame
# Sample operation
```

data.set = rbind(dataset1);
airports <- c('ATL', 'LAX', 'ORD', 'DFW', 'JFK', 'SFO', 'CLT', 'LAS', 'PHX')
origData1 <- subset(data.set, DEST %in% airports & ORIGIN %in% airports)

# Select data.frame to be sent to the output Dataset port
maml.mapOutputPort("origData1");

After doing the coding select only the columns required. After selecting the columns remove the rows that contain "" or empty string or NA in the column.

The next step is to split the data into 70% of Sample data for training the model and 30% of test data to test the final modals accuracy.

Machine Learning

After spliting the data run the flow generated. Now add the two class logistic regression and Train Model work flow. Here in train model we add ARR_DEL15 as the column to be predicted.

After Training the model click on score the model and send the test data to the score model flow. This will use the trained model and predict the test data.

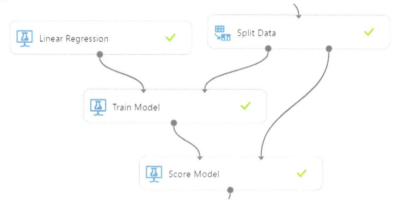

The output of the score model is connected to evaluate model which is used for visualization. The complete flow diagram is shown below.

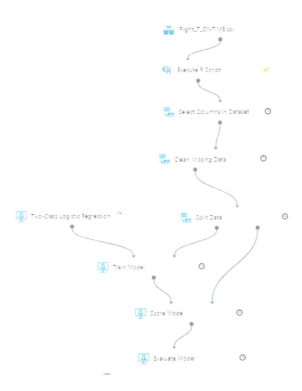

The final step is to visualize the results of the confusion matrix to see how well our model performed.

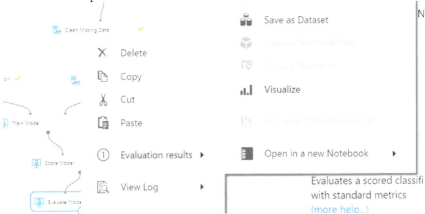

The confusion matrix shows that True positive, True Negative, False Positive and False Negagive. Here Positive means 1 which means flight got delayed and Negative means 0 which means flight did not get delayed.

True Positive	False Negative	Accuracy	Precision
1839	704	0.880	0.808

False Positive	True Negative	Recall	F1 Score
436	6559	0.723	0.763

Positive Label	Negative Label
1	0

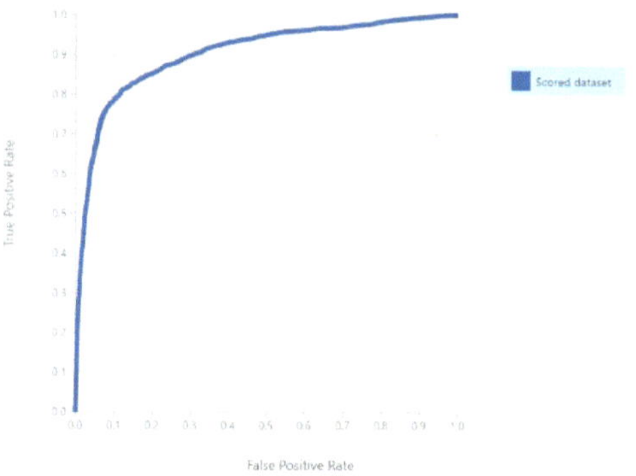

True positive and True Negative means that the system has detected correctly. False Positive and False Negative means that the system has detected incorrectly. Thus we get the confusion matrix for Azure Machine Learning. We can use different Algorithms available under Machine Learning tab > Initialize Model. The end result of evaluate model will vary, it could display histogram, confusion matrix or some other depending on the Model. The graph above shows that if the line obtained tends towards 1 then it means that the model is more accurate, but if the line tends to fall below the center line then the model is less accurate and hence we have to change the algorithm.

◢ 🔲 Machine Learning

    ▷ Evaluate

    ◢ Initialize Model

        ▷ Anomaly Detection

        ▷ Classification

        ▷ Clustering

        ▷ Regression

In order to run Mahout we require Hadoop Name node and Data nodes and Yarn resource manager to be running. Same as given in Chapter 2. Here the left side shows the [Hadoop-Cl1 machine] Master and right side shows [Hadoop-Cl2 machine] Slave with JPS, Name node and Data node running.

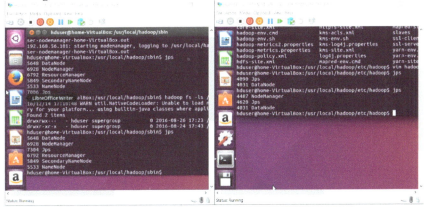

There are some prerequisites before running Mahout, like installation of the packages. Download and extract the latest Mahout distribution on the master machine. We are ready to execute all the algorithms that comes along with the Mahout distribution.

ABOUT THE AUTHOR

Srinivas V V is a Software Developer, Research scholar who has published articles, journals, research, conference and white papers on topics related to distributed systems, cloud and grid computing, computer architecture. He has presented lectures and workshops on various Universities across India. He has worked on data warehousing, web and mobile applications. The author holds a Master's degree from National Institute of Technology Trichy, India.

www.ingramcontent.com/pod-product-compliance
Lightning Source LLC
LaVergne TN
LVHW012316070326
832902LV00001BA/22